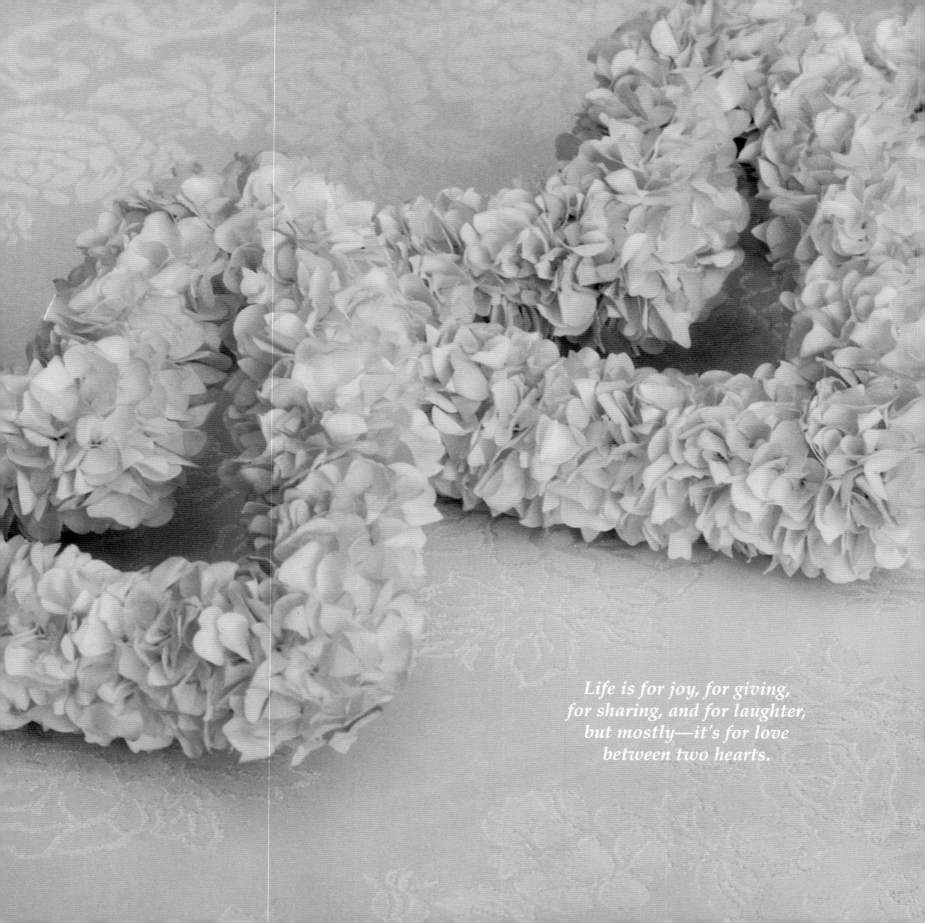

*Life is for joy, for giving,
for sharing, and for laughter,
but mostly—it's for love
between two hearts.*

Wedding Style

Sy Snarr

Sterling Publishing Co., Inc. New York
A Sterling/Chapelle Book

Chapelle, Limited

Owner: Jo Packham

Editor: Caroll Schreeve

Editorial Consultant: Brad Mee

Art Director: Karla Haberstich

Design/Layout: Brad Mee

Staff: Areta Bingham, Kass Burchett, Ray Cornia, Jill Dahlberg, Marilyn Goff, Holly Hollingsworth, Susan Jorgensen, Barbara Milburn, Karmen Quinney, Cindy Stoeckl, Kim Taylor, Sara Toliver, Desirée Wybrow

If you have any questions or comments, please contact:
Chapelle, Ltd., Inc., P.O. Box 9252 Ogden, UT 84409
(801) 621-2777 • FAX (801) 621-2788
• e-mail: chapelle@chapelleltd.com • web site: www.chapelleltd.com

Library of Congress Cataloging-in-Publication Data Available

Snarr, Sy.
     Wedding style / Sy Snarr.
     p. cm.
     Includes index.
     ISBN 0-8069-8283-7
       1. Weddings--Planning. 2. Wedding etiquette. 3. Weddings--Equipment
        and supplies.
   I. Title.

HQ745 .S56 2002
395.2'2--dc21

2002070789

10 9 8 7 6 5 4 3 2 1

Published by Sterling Publishing Co., Inc.
387 Park Avenue South, New York, NY 10016
© 2002 by Sy Snarr
Distributed in Canada by Sterling Publishing
% Canadian Manda Group, One Atlantic Avenue, Suite 105
Toronto, Ontario, Canada M6K 3E7
Distributed in Great Britain and Europe by Chrysalis Books
64 Brewery Road, London N7 9NT, England
Distributed in Australia by Capricorn Link (Australia) Pty. Ltd.
P.O. Box 704, Windsor, NSW 2756, Australia
Printed in China
All Rights Reserved

Sterling ISBN 0-8069-8283-7

To Thee I....

Wed

Contents

Introduction   8

Classic Style   10

Formal   12
Romantic   28
Sophisticated   50

Natural Style   60

Seasonal   62
spring   64
summer   72
autumn   78
winter   82
Outdoor   90
Country   96

Spirited Style   106

Ranch   110
Family   124
Eclectic   132

Acknowledgments   142
Appreciation   143
Index   143

Introduction

Weddings

Weddings conjure up romance in the union of two people in love. Celebrating their commitment may take many style forms that embrace basic components of the wedding concept: elegance, or at least quality of the highest sort within even an informal theme, and fine photography to record each special ritual and moment.

Style

Delightful surprise elements styled to enhance a decorative theme are features of today's weddings. These style details support the wedding concept, be it formal, informal, or abounding in imaginative attitude and personality.

The bride selects her photography style as she does every other aspect of her wedding. Her photo album should be appropriate to the tone of the ceremony and reception, with attention given to style detail in formal or informal poses, candid precious moments, and bridal party and couple compositions.

Classic Style

The wedding in classic style employs traditional formal elements symmetrically arranged. Classy sophistication is apparent in every nuance of style detail from wedding party ensembles to the decorative embellishment of sacred-vow and secular-reception spaces.

Natural Style

A natural style is unpretentious and more relaxed. The bride may incorporate nostalgic country touches for a charming wedding and a reception with dancing held out-of-doors.

Spirited Style

More frequently now, eclectic weddings exhibit the bride's and groom's unique personalities with an expressive departure from tradition. Themes of a creative nature delight wedding guests with the unexpected in imaginative abandon styled into wedding attire, ceremony and reception location, approach to appetizing food presentation, and beauty in theme floral design.

Classic style

The photographer has the opportunity and responsibility to isolate the bride's and groom's wedding day to the symbolic heart of their bond, in a spontaneous gesture or loving look, or a posed moment.

Here, a formal pose becomes more intimate when the focus is on the groom's arms embracing his bride. She returns her acceptance of their commitment with a relaxed touching of their fingers amid her flowers. The beauty and power here go beyond the style of her gown and his tuxedo, the bridal bouquet, or the sparkling diamond. Like an artist, the photographer presents the simple honesty of two people in love through the hands they will use to nurture one another for a satisfying lifetime.

Breaking with tradition that calls for faces, the risk the photographer takes is to take our breath with "just enough" detail to tell a love story. Its universal quality is symbolic of every wedding pair. Such an exquisite focus expresses more than marriage between a specific man and woman, but the timeless quality of the state of matrimony itself.

FORMAL

For the love of it all, people in love go to great effort and expense to make a lifetime memory out of a moment—the one when they say "I do."

Formal weddings are traditional in approach. The wedding day is all about pairs. People and objects are arranged in careful rows or classical groupings of symmetrical elegance; colors are matched to perfection; stunning bride and groom cakes and satin gowns to complement tuxedos catch every eye; elaborate hairstyles beneath veils are whispered about; and breathtaking floral arrangements symbolize a blossoming romance. Selected music enhances candlelit buffet tables and fragrant centerpieces. Guests are transported to mythic days when the handsome prince rode up on a white steed and swept the swooning princess off her balcony. He took her away to his mysterious castle for a beautiful wedding and a sumptuous feast.

Today's formal weddings conform in matters of photography to traditional marriage ceremony pictorials of the past. Wedding party individuals are grouped in matching "wings" on either side and perhaps in rows behind and low in front of the bridal pair. Settings frame the loving couple at the church where the ceremony is held, or perhaps on a grand staircase in a hotel or private home, a lush lawn with an archway or symmetrically placed potted palms or balustrades are typical for classical photos. Portraits of the couple— or her alone—happen on the steps of a church; before a velvet or lace-draped backdrop, an ivy-twined lattice, or a blooming garden or lily pond; beneath a flower-bedecked archway; or on a charming garden bridge or balcony.

The style of a formal wedding before 200 guests includes precise details from colors to fabric choices, jewelry, gloves, hats and hair ornaments, hairstyles for the men and women of the party, boutonnieres and bouquets, cummerbund and satin shoes, and ring bearer's pillow. Cakes and flowers are perfection. The bride's choices reign supreme on her life-dream day, or evening.

Formal weddings may have their surprising moments but they settle on the strength of symmetrical focal points and thoughtfully conceived style details. Formality is quintessential stability, symbolically reflecting the wedding couple's lifetime commitment. Classic statements of sophistication exude simplicity. Cakes for the bride and the groom are sculpted works of art. Tiers are festooned with frosting or satin ribbons, artfully arranged blossoms and foliage in the bride's choice of wedding colors, accented with crystal. The more formal the wedding, the more restrained the colors—black and white or entirely white.

Regal wedding cakes star at the reception. Creative nouvelle cake designers employ colored and sculpted frostings to form cascading flowers. Cast and pleated paper embellishments and beads are sometimes used along with candles, ice sculptures, and fresh floral arrangements to enhance them. The ethereal spire of white is a heavenly symbol of spiritual commitment and high style; while if there is a groom's cake it is usually styled to symbolize an earth-bound weighty stability, emphasizing practical matters of the heart. The contrast of the traditional white-tiered cake and the groom's often dark chocolate one is a play of feminine and masculine ideas and energy in style details. The groom's cake should be his favorite, perhaps applesauce, a simple or elaborately sculpted dark or German chocolate, a pound cake, or even a pumpkin cheesecake heavy with nuts and dried fruit.

Classical architectural structures make elegant statements framing the wedding couple, as with the arch to the right. Though the style is traditional formal attire, their pose is intimate with a light touch. The atypical detail of pine branches with lilies for the bride and her attendants, below, is a style accent surprise that makes this bride's wedding taste unique and memorable.

The formal cake at right is sophisticated in style. Limiting the colors to white and gold emphazises the simple beauty of the concept that is completed with gold pedestal supports. The calla lily blossoms are repeated sculptural forms in frosting with elegant and surprising touches of gold leaf shapes applied directly onto the smoothly frosted tiers.

Formal receptions celebrate uniting two people amid the beauty and fragrance of roses, the time-lessly expressive flower of love, or lilies. Add candles to an already glowing event. If the reception is held out-of-doors, a breezy atmosphere need not curtail your use of candles, as many as can be arranged safely, in levels. Plan for a variety of transparent containers among flowers. Employ open-at-the-top glass chimneys. These allow the candles to breathe properly for a steady flame, but prevent too rapid burning, scorching of flower petals, and wafting of smoke, causing discomfort for seated guests.

Make your style goal a delight at every place guests will pause. At left, crystal and lace are lovely heirloom touches. Votive candles nested in groups of clear glass bowls add low shimmer in a buffet arrangement while they reflect sparkles upward. At right, they illuminate edibles against a surprising backdrop of fresh green grass at table height. Below, a chest at the reception entry features guest book, photos of the couple, and gifts for the guests to take.

Make every ordinary day special...somehow. — Jo Packham

Arrange for an abundance of colors and textures in hors d'oeuvres. The more formal the occasion, the more styled the food. Each nibble shape should look dainty and "fussed over."

Individual dessert "bites" invite conversation as well as delight the palette. Mix arrangements of sweets in individual papers for easy handling by best-dressed guests. A variety of crunchy items, frosted petit fours, glazed fruit tarts, layered cookies in theme shapes, tiny sand tarts extruded in beautiful scallop shapes from pastry tips are expected on formal buffet tables. Top with shaved chocolate in dark as well as white, but account for the temperature. You want nothing on your tables that will begin to wilt, sweat, or have saggy frosting.

Well-styled food presentations should look as beautiful at the end of the reception as they do when the first guest is served. Accounting for long lines of attendees plays an important part in your formal food selections. Ideally, seat guests quickly, use catered service, or limit your list and plan for self-serve.

The chancel step setting at left is ideal for a formal portrait. Its purposefully darkened background with subdued details enhances the bride and groom.

A garden kiss, an initialed cake, lovely! Double weddings, as above, are twice as dramatic for two couples. Planning for photography must include a secluded indoor or courtyard place, apart from the amateur photographers who'll be overeager to record the event. Note the two different bridal gown designs.

Formal elegance in symmetrical design assures the beautiful simplicity in an arrangement of a vase of ruby roses flanked by a pair of commanding candle-holders. The chunky, rather than taper-style, candles center the focus on the roses. Lower-grouped votives repeat the symmetrical pairing the glass panes reflect.

The bride, below, epitomizes simple as enchanting. Her dark hair is styled to feature her gathered-lace veil and her lovely skin tone and dark lashes. The lack of distracting jewelry keeps the focus on this pretty bride's serenity. Her ruby-toned roses match her lipstick—just enough. Classic pose and photographer's lighting styled from the left—the lacy veil side—add tasteful drama to her demure downcast eyes.

27

ROMANTIC

*R*omance, just the word brings to mind sweet sentiment, thoughtful gestures, and beautiful expressions of love. This style in weddings is unpretentious, nostalgic, and very romantic in every element. The attention to detail on the bridal bouquet pictured here includes seed pearls carefully secured on floral wire to the center of stephanotis blossoms. The dewy result is light softly captured in "droplets" among the yellow roses, an unexpected delight. Plump golden rose blossoms paired with lavender hydrangeas play the complementary colors of purple and yellow to one another in an unusual and particularly pleasing array. The bride's lace sleeves set the theme of tiny flower blossom accents from bouquets to tables.

Old-world formalism relaxes in the romantic style. It's all about sentiment by blending meaningful keepsakes and mementos of family and friends with the new and fresh in style. Romantic style gives the couple opportunities to honor marriage traditions from their separate families, while creating memorable new ones to be handed down to their own children. It may mean refitting a precious gown or headpiece, securing the groom's tie or the bride's veil with a treasured diamond stickpin, or the bride wearing an antique locket while the groom sports an heirloom watch fob on his tuxedo cummerbund. Nostalgic romance may entail sentimental to creative fantasy, or Cinderella to atmospheric theme qualities. Romantic style may be simple or fussy, down-to-earth homey or elaborate, but it will always be soft and at ease. Romantic weddings and receptions may be spontaneous, charming, country, ranch, or garden affairs, all out-of-doors. The bride's sense of style brings every aspect of the day's celebration activities into one package of beauty and happiness to be treasured by all.

and spoiling her family and friends for the sheer delight of it is enough to keep any bride up nights planning and creating. From the guest books to the photo albums, the focal points to display them, and the personal gifts from her to her wedding party, the selection of even the tiniest embellishments is intended to express the dreams of two people in love. A candle glows in a dish of pearls, crystal, and roses, on the bridal attendants' vanity.

In every wedding, it's the little things that enhance the memories. In romantic weddings, possible theme motifs are often the reason a bride selected a romantic theme in the first place. Making everything pretty and unique is part of what makes her wedding day so special. Expressing her taste and personality, sharing her dreams of the life-style she and her fiancé want to have,

A pair of doves perch on a dish filled with Wedding Rice® reminding guests of the special nature of the day for the wedding couple. The pair of cupids embroidered on the ring pillow could be decorating a vintage heirloom or a handmade gift from a member of the bride or groom's family.

Bring "style" items for themes out of your trunks and closets, off the bed, and out of cupboards or borrow them from willing family and friends.

An inexpensive and delightful idea for guest favors is personalized paper weights. The glass hearts, lower right, can be purchased at craft and variety stores for a reasonable price. They act as little magnifiers of whatever words or paper designs you cut to fit the heart shapes and affix to the bottoms.

Ideas to be lettered in elegant calligraphy might be the bride's and groom's names and wedding date, the individual names of the guests receiving the favors at their plates, brief messages from or favorite quotes of the newlyweds, or snippets of romantic poetry.

Romantic wedding receptions may be understated or styled "over the top." Nature elements of fresh flowers, lush grass, doves, seashells, music drifting gently among the guests, fountains adding their soft notes . . . sweet. Glue pairs of seashells, sandwich style with the bulb between them, to strings of Christmas lights for the charming dining effect at right. Select glue that withstands prolonged bulb heat; the bulb will not be able to be changed later.

Evening wedding receptions renew our love affair with shimmering candlelight and twinkling tea lights. This bride wished to dine by catered courses at draped and theme-decorated tables, fragrant with flowers, then dance the night away in her dress-up attire.

Every bride has a style.

A romantic mood is spontaneous, natural; it may be dreamy in atmosphere. The bride may opt for a wreath of flower blossoms in lieu of a formal pearl-encrusted headpiece and trailing veil. Her hair may be softly curled as in a Rosetti painting, or naturally flowing. In understated makeup, she may swath herself in lace, ruffles, wispy organdy, or satin trimmed in cascading ribbons, and embroidery.

The unique goblets for the newlywed's toast, below, were commissioned works of art. They will be brought out by the couple for anniversaries, Valentine's Day, and other special occasions. Crystal or ordinary glassware, silver or enameled goblets can be personalized with engraving. Or as take-home favors, wedding-guest goblets can have beads with the names of the bride and groom strung on wires looped around their stems.

 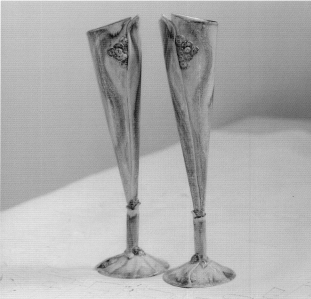 

Keep colors of small items closely related to enhance their beauty. The warm arrangement, above left, glows with gold, rich peach, and sienna. Patterns and colors relate in the goblet, the bottle of wine in a cover, the gold edge on the plate, beaded napkin ring, to the damask cloth and tiny frame.

Dining guests feel regal seated in chairs "dressed" and sashed in taffeta. A single rose tucked into the back of each has a tiny corsage water container, to keep it fresh, at right. A silk flower could be used as well as a tassel, loops of beads, or ribbons with a charm pendant keyed to the style theme.

A focal-point display near the guest book features the bride's love of pearls, and beaded and fresh flowers used to enhance a stack of her favorite classics.

A white-on-white cake is especially snowlike for a winter wedding. Grapes, roses, and swags with leaf shapes in all-white frosting make an elegant statement for a classic cake in the romantic style. The formal grapes resemble pearls or sculpted white marble.

Seashells are a naturally romantic theme for weddings, whether the beach is at the edge of the reception area or thousands of miles away. Shell shapes and colors were a favorite of the romantic Victorians who used them to embellish everything from architecture to china and jewelry. Here, toile fabrics for table coverings and napkins echo shell colors, while the shells themselves embellish gift packages, chairs, flatware, and napkin rings. Elsewhere they are "arranged" freely on tables and in potted patio plants, as they might be found on the beach. Tea lights in the shapes of shells are delightful when strung about a seating area, at an entry, or near the champagne table.

We "shell" always be good to each other. —Carroll Shreeve

Delicate designs marry well with flowers, beads, and lace. The vintage hair ornaments at right, with their beaded loops, accompany embroidered hankies and lace-embellished sheer beautifully. Personal keepsakes like these may be treasured items of the bride's mother, grandmother, or godmother. To replicate the idea, simple picks and combs may be purchased and then enhanced with beads strung on looped wires.

The candle, below, with its trailing vine and flower surface treatment is at home with a bead and ribbon "neckace" to create a stylish focal point. The newlywed's head table at the rehearsal dinner or wedding reception would be aglow with a styled row of them.

I tell you my dreams, and while you are listening to me, I see them come true —Alan Jay Lerner

Capturing the prince of a groom ready to sweep the princess of a bride down into his waiting arms, after their romantic carriage ride, is a charming moment worth staging for the photographer. The fairy-tale wedding is complete.

Romance crackles with mystery when the bride sweeps by, partially obscured by her wispy veil. When the veil is cathedral length and trails well behind her, perhaps assisted over a path by her bridesmaids or young train bearers, the fantasy is especially memorable.

The bride, at left, has the long hairstyle, row of back bodice buttons, and bare arms and shoulders that add to the romantic style details of her veiled appearance. These are what movie weddings try to emulate and never quite can because the air of a "real" wedding is alive with genuine excitement and love.

As at right, a place setting for the reception can combine a variety of old and new elements. A family quilt could serve as an elegant tablecloth for the head table. Bring out a marvelously mismatched collection of plates, flatware, napkins, napkin rings, and stemware with a flair. Harmonize them with complementary gift-box favors.

Beaded embellishments are stylish seasonally or all year round. The delicate beauty of the purple Aurora Borealis butterfly at right accents clothing, hair ornaments, or becomes "jewelry" for a gift box.

Echo the elegance of a grand hotel, even on a tight budget. The most practical of chairs, perhaps the folding variety, look fabulous with a lace slip cover over their backs. Theme-decorate with clouds of sheer and ribbon and the splash and fragrance of lovely flowers to make a church hall sparkle. Unique cakes "bloom" with trailing vine accents, too.

Tiny bejeweled frames with the wedding couple's portrait inside and their names and wedding date on the back make romantic guest gifts at each pretty table set-ting, or use as centerpiece art.

Silver nosegays that hold the most delicate of fresh or silk violets or lily-of-the-valley blossoms are lovely for each attendant to carry and keep as a gift from the bride.

A heart in love with beauty never grows old.

The concept of a tiered wedding cake can be taken beyond a beautiful baked-and-frosted focal point.

Left and above, a series of size-graduated round boxes have been covered with lovely pastel fabrics and stacked as miniature traditional wedding-style cakes.

Their tiers have been embellished with scallops of folded and fanned ribbon, yards of textured trim, and ribbon roses for a stunning series of centerpieces to use on either end of the buffet table and at the gift or guest book. The amazing creation above was fashioned to be used in place of the ring bearer's pillow. Note the diamond wedding band secured with pastel ribbon cushioned beautifully in the top tier.

A cone of lacy pastel vellum or handmade paper makes a lovely holder for a few blossoms to spill from on a table, on the vanity in the ladies' room, or where champagne will be served for the newlywed's toast.

Another idea for the paper or vellum cone is to make enough that each guest is given one. Fill with rose petals, in lieu of the traditional shower of rice, to be thrown at the departure of the newlyweds from the church or following the dance, as they leave for their honeymoon. Display the cones in a vintage metal cola or milk rack sprayed with pretty paint in the bride's colors. Or stuff them gently into baskets, or brightly colored wheelbarrows. The waiting display is ideal for a camera-ready focal point keyed to candid portraits.

49

SOPHISTICATED

*O*nly the sophisticated approach to the classic style of wedding is as challenging for the bride to plan as the formal one. The sophisticated bride is confident of her personal sense of style and sure of her ability to "pull it off" in myriad details. Though she may well retain many mode strategies of traditional formal planning, such as symmetrical arrangements, gowns, veils, tuxedos, engraved invitations and announcements, and formal poses for her photography, she is likely to be more adventurous. The sophisticated bride will explore asymmetrical balance, emphasize a white-on-white, ivory with pastels, or black and white wedding color choice. She will probably select lilies or ruby red roses, or the unusual as opposed to a sweet and delicate pink rose theme, for example. If she has the figure for it, she will choose the dramatic fitted gown, perhaps in strapless or a more revealing front or back style. She is a daring bride!

The sophisticated wedding and reception will be elegant in every detail, but may have fewer sentimental touches than the matrimonial events of the romantic bride. An air of being timeless, worldly but tasteful, utterly above all things mundane exudes from the sophisticated bride who delights her guests with "over the top" extravagance intentionally restrained. She will never be outrageous but will definitely be "classy." Diamonds will sparkle, as will crystal, silver, pewter, and platinum. Sparkle will be on her person, at the wedding and at the sit-down dinner at her reception. High fashion will shine from the wedding-party ensembles, her table and floral decorations, to her magnificent cake, or many cakes!

The sophisticated bride may exhibit "minimalist" tendencies with simplicity that is classic, or she may plan for an abundance of detail that stops just short of overwhelming her guests. In all things she will know when "just enough" is "just right." Her sense of drama will play an important role in how she styles her attention to every wedding-day component from the guest book to her veil. Her sense of adventure will be apparent in her delight in surprising touches that call attention to the finest in quality of guest comfort and pleasure in her day.

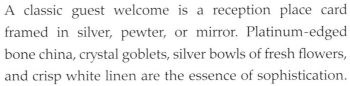

A classic guest welcome is a reception place card framed in silver, pewter, or mirror. Platinum-edged bone china, crystal goblets, silver bowls of fresh flowers, and crisp white linen are the essence of sophistication.

A simple bouquet in all one color of flowers, perhaps with ribbon-wrapped stems is as sophisticatedly simple as a single flower "garniture" on a guest plate. Guests take the flower home to press as a memento.

For those who can afford it, a sophisticated reception in a grand hotel or country-club ballroom is bound to be a memorable affair. Chandeliers and opulent architecture add their classic grace to the upscale festivities. A catered dining experience with beautiful appointments for place settings, dramatic cake presentation, champagne toasts, and a small orchestra delight newlyweds and wedding guests alike. Photography will be suitably classic with luxurious surroundings as a background setting. The bride can add fabulous style details of her own, as long as she assigns trusted loved ones to assist in their retrieval and return to her. Each table can be embellished with different monogrammed napkin rings, beaded centerpieces, or her heirloom linens.

An angel for me and an angel for you . . .

A wedding cake in sophisticated style is often white on white or dressed in muted frosting colors, with scrolls of lacy detail and beaded in silver nonpareils.

Crystal, white candles, and long-stemmed calla lilies, all arranged in a stately arrangement are dazzling in their sophistication. At left, white and ivory candles and simple white china are classic elegance played against the lush grass, food, and roses. White, pale yellow, crystal and repeated forms are sophisticated at right.

The sophisticated bride with a spirit of adventure may dare to take a few liberties with her styling details. Perhaps she will carry but one lily or a single rose. She may choose to wear a long gown and a tiara, but may ask to be photographed barefoot—contessa style—bordering on the romantic or the natural wedding style, but walking the edge.

And though classic symmetry is linear or circular, she may arrange her attendants and herself in a perfect circle, but then send her photographer to the balcony to shoot from above. The result is a surprising photo album memory that is classic and sophisticated in her style.

The only lasting beauty is the beauty of the heart — Rumi

Natural style

Whether the natural style wedding is held indoors or outside, elements of nature will be emphasized in the styling details of wedding and reception. The natural bride enjoys her departure from formality in a relaxed attitude, but her planning may bridge romantic and sophisticated classicism with her desire to draw in her love of the out-of-doors. Particularly if nature loving is a life-style choice she and her husband-to-be will share for a lifetime, the natural in style will appeal to both of the newlyweds.

Even indoors, the natural style is lively with styling details that are easy to notice. Hair will be similar to softly romantic styles per-haps, or it may be wispy, uncontrived into some ornate style, and flowing naturally. This bride may choose a crown of flowers, with or without a veil, or perhaps only a hair ornament. She may choose a bouquet spiked with twigs, or a bouffant dress covered in embroidered flowers, rather than a svelte gown encrusted with pearls. Her reception style may employ fruits and vegetables and regional delicacies for her guest treats. Her gifts will be natural. Whatever the details the natural bride chooses to emphasize in her wedding and reception, the beautiful touches the guests will notice will be taken from nature and her love of all things fresh.

SEASONAL

$\mathscr{F}$or the bride and groom who live in a region where seasonal changes are dramatic, styles are chosen in terms of appropriate color and available flowers for their wedding and reception will be clear quickly. For those who have unlimited financial resources and can order imported flowers, perhaps only color selection limitations will come into their decision making. For most brides who choose to be married in the spring, traditional spring colors and flowers will determine their wedding theme and style. Pastels and leaf- and flower-bud tints will prevail.

The summer wedding is warm with promise, whether held indoors or out on the lawn. Flowers are in their prime blooming season and colors are multihued. Temperatures in most climates present opportunities for the ceremony and the reception to be held out-of-doors. In addition, summer evenings are comfortable enough for the moon, stars, and fireflies to remind guests that nature was the first romantic. Natural brides take every advantage of what nature provides.

In autumn, the rich colors of harvesttime come into play with nature's bounty. The warmth of ripe wheat, pumpkins, red maple leaves, golden ginko and aspen leaves, and berries that ripen in the fall burst with goodness and color. Historically as auspicious a time for weddings as the promise of spring, autumn weddings can have a unique styling echoed from nature's harvest.

The winter wedding calls to mind snow queens and ice palaces. If snowflakes and ice crystals can be warm ideas, it's all because of love's influence. Winter isn't snowy everywhere, of course, but the concepts of cozy intimacy made necessary by the cold in some climates, make for a unique twist on weddings. White as a color has a starring role in the winter wedding, with all of its theme elements, including the month of February's contribution with Valentine's Day. Most regions host holly berries and leaves, evergreen boughs, and ruby-red roses for "flowers."

Because the seasons of the year lend themselves so well to wedding and reception themes, aligning the date of the wedding with its season is a success in the making. The actual elements the bride puts together may be conceptual ideas, as with the tulip candles at left, rather than, or in addition to, employing fresh tulip blossoms in her floral arrangements. Her flowers may also be the "real thing." Whatever approach the bride takes to make a visual statement of the seasonal wedding style, it is just naturally going to involve items taken from nature.

spring

The spring seasonal style of a natural wedding is imbued with the promise of good things to come for the wedding couple. Symbolically, as the metaphor for beginnings, seed planting, and the building of nests, there couldn't be a more natural time to enjoy a wedding and reception. For the couple coming together to covenant their commitment for seasons to come, the spring wedding celebrates nature as well as love.

Natural wedding styles give the bride an opportunity to be unpretentious and close to the cycles of the seasons. Her bridal clothing choices may be as elegant as desired, but they will be comfortable for every member of the wedding party. Simple hair treatments, unrestricting dresses, and bouquets with the appearance of having just been plucked from a garden are the styling ideals of the natural approach that appears in spring weddings.

Love is the only flower that grows and blossoms without the aid of the seasons. — *Kahlil Gibran*

The floral design shown here incorporates evergreen branches and ruby-toned twigs with blossoms that are not fully open—a sure sign of spring.

Where evergreens and glossy-leaved plants such as camellias and magnolia trees are prevalent, combine them with lilacs or spring berries.

Flowers presented in out-of-the-ordinary ways make lovely weddings more exciting. At near left, the cut stems of the bride's tulip and lily bouquet have been wrapped with ribbon and exposed for a "just picked" appearance that celebrates spring.

The bride, far left, has a sweet and fragrant touch to the back of her bodice where her maid of honor secured a dance corsage of her wedding flowers.

Above, the bride shares her bouquet with her blossom-wreathed flower girl. All are fresh-flower interpretations of the spring wedding theme. If the freedom of no fluttering veil or flowers to weigh heavily on a natural hairstyle is an idea that appeals to some brides, a beaded hair-comb ornament may be the elegant solution. Wear vintage or create one!

69

A natural wedding theme for the spring season is always about freshness in nature. Lemons and long-stemmed iris blossoms combined here enhance one another with color, texture, fragrance, and imagined "flavor." Arbor roses float with tea candles in a spring flood of fresh water and bike baskets, or wheelbarrows boast lavender and roses.

The natural spring wedding doesn't require a stunning heirloom container for any focal point. Plastic, pressed tin or aluminum, basket, or recycled can may serve imaginatively, and practically, where silver, bronze, pewter, crystal, and copper play the role of container in a formal wedding. These florals are relaxed and no less elegant.

Stuffing shiny new buckets with sand for stability and crushed paper, before adding sphagnum moss, flowers, lemons, or early vegetables is an ideal way to say spring. Keeping other wedding colors simple allows the natural items to take center stage, visually as well as symbolically for the natural wedding-reception decorative style.

summer

Summer receptions beg to be held outdoors. The time the bride chooses will depend upon the most comfortable time of day or evening for the location. Always consider breezes between buildings or mountains that occur in cycles, afternoon sprinkles that are quite predictable, and other weather-related concerns that tents or shelters can minimize.

Not only is it important to make guests comfortable with seating, but to assure that everyone can see and hear the various rituals that are so important to the celebration. When the wedding itself is to be held out-of-doors, microphones may be necessary. Their required wires must be camouflaged and handled in a safe manner so that no one trips over them or dislodges them at a tender moment. Styling a wedding out-of-doors is for the adventurous and those who prepare for most inclement weather possibilities.

Summer food selections are laced with color and textures that emphasize the freshest produce used in surprising combinations. Below, center, cold salmon poses with cucumber "scales" and a strawberry in its mouth. To the left and right, buffet tables display beautiful entrées and desserts. Various levels of presentation for each plate, styled to complement one another, create a pleasing tablescape of visual as well as tasty delights.

Take advantage of architectural elements and decorative containers in outdoor reception settings. At right, the existing kumquat tree makes a more powerful style statement with the addition of fresh grapes, purple plums, and lemons. The same fruit items were used on the guest tables in similar focal points with different, lower design approaches—to account for guests being able to make eye contact. Terra-cotta pots, surrounded by green fabric that matches the grapes, are studded with artichokes for color and texture, eggplant to reflect purple plums, lemons, and votives.

Summertime is wonderfully warm, making afternoon outdoor wedding receptions a comfortable joy for everyone. Flowers are at the height of their blooming glory if a garden setting is available. Celebratory gatherings are preferably held in late afternoon when the sun has past its zenith and natural light and shadow set a more romantic mood. It's a lazy time for bees, too. However, if the time of day required for the exchange of wedding vows means holding the reception when it's still quite hot, which in some regions lasts into early evening, do provide tents or garden shelters for the guests. Take advantage of the shady sides of buildings for food and champagne tables, flower displays, guest seating, and photo settings.

The bridal gown style, at left, was chosen especially for a summer wedding. Tiny flowers, embroidered in soft summer colors, are perfect to complement the vows exchanged out-of-doors. The bride chose her bouquet flowers to complement those in her gown, making sure both were styled with trailing vines.

It is guest- and bride-friendly to make sure best-dressed is not most uncomfortable when dining. Late afternoon receptions make evening dancing a lovely transition following a sit-down dinner, toasts to the bride and groom, and time for the bride and groom to change into their traveling attire. Natural summer weddings feature clothing that moves with ease.

autumn

The warm tones of autumn, derived from harvest colors of grapes to grains, set a memorable palette for the fall bride. Colors are robust, as though they've absorbed all the sunshine they can hold. Golds, yellows, oranges, rich ruby reds, and variations on purple and sienna in floral designs seem perfect to complement happy couples and glowing candlelight. Centerpieces in the autumn mood may be as simple as terra-cotta pots stuffed with a bounty of flowers. Or fill miniature "harvest" baskets with favors wrapped in fall-colored papers. Tie with the bride's colors in ribbon or organdy and surround with votives. Paper cornucopias spilling grapes, late roses, or just their petals, are lovely on guest tables.

A picture-perfect cake for an autumn wedding theme is at right. Grapes in red, purple, and yellow green are the cake's main style features. Sculpted leaves, beautiful cluster shapes and lush colors, not to mention sweet aroma, make the grapes elegant embellishments for a frosting concept that displays a minimum of pastry-tip art to transition between the tiers. They could be "frosted" with sugar as table decorations to complement the cake, since grapes are best harvested after the first frost. Decorative options are clusters of rose hips, walnuts or pecans in their shells, oak leaves with their acorns, the golden fan-shaped leaves of the ornamental ginko tree, red and gold maple leaves, and white, gold, rust, or purple chrysanthemums.

Why not break the single, multitiered wedding cake tradition for a focal-point grouping of several cakes? For a wedding reception with a lengthy guest list, consider how several stunning cakes arranged in a variety of heights would make not only a fabulous presentation, but would allow serving all of your guests efficiently. Several caterers can cut and serve the various cakes simultaneously. The cakes need not match except in mood and style. Note the variety of piped diamond-and-swag frosting embellishments as you move from cake to cake.

winter

Winter weddings have a special sparkle. The drama of chill and snow adds a crisp note to any winter style in cold climates. Recalling the snow princess from *Grimm's Fairy Tales* or *Snow White*, the beauty of red roses against white gowns, snowflakes, and as at left, a white fur-edged hooded cape—well, the style is breathtaking. If the wedding is in February, a Valentine's Day theme of red hearts, pink, and white with black for a theme is sophisticated. Valentine's Day is, other than June, the most popular season for a wedding. It will be romantic, whether formally sophisticated or tuned to nature's chill. Icy style details will reign for a memorable theme reception.

Since metals that sparkle increase the drama of ice and snowflake concepts in a winter theme, emphasize those qualities with silver, pewter, and crystal details. Shimmer is for winter. The more sophisticated the bride's taste, the more styled she'll want her wedding ensemble, her attendants, the groomsmen, and her floral arrangements and formal photography.

The rich tones of dark chocolate—or the pristine white of white chocolate—are perfect wedding cake accompaniments to the winter reception. The tiered cake at right seems sculpted from fudge, and its crowning ornaments of winter berries and red and gold roses are all the more dramatic when reflected by a gilt-framed mirror. Echo it in the table floral styling.

Love lies hidden in every rose. —Alfred Noyes

The Valentine's Day wedding calls for red, white, and pink hearts in creative treatments with a high romance value, as limitless as the bride's imagination. Hearts, lips, cupids, and bows star as centerpiece "lollipops," reception favors or place-card holders. Add roses, white flowers, white china, red- or pink-trimmed table linens, chair back decorations, theme gifts, and guest books.

Since Valentine's Day will come again and again, just as the wedding couple's anniversaries will, investing in some special permanent decorative items is a reasonable choice to make. The porcelain pastry serving piece above, for example, has a slotted design to its edge. Not only can it be brought out for anniversaries and future Valentine's Day celebrations, with red and green ribbons, it's perfect for Christmas, spring colors for Easter, etc.

From lavish to modest, Valentine's Day wedding and reception decorations are delightful to style. Hearts abound in candies and pretzels, cutouts, and jewels.

Rows of fringed trim, inside a vintage frame antiqued with red, make a charming conversation starter for those who stop to enjoy pictures of the newlyweds.

Photographs, tiny packages, cards from well wishers, and tiny romantic remembrances are held with small red clips for a Valentine's Day wedding reception. Nearby, a pair of faux wedding rings secured with ribbons to a red-satin heart, ccmbine with roses to carry out "the most romantic day of the year" theme.

OUTDOOR

$\mathscr{O}$utdoor wedding and reception plans are the most natural of all the styles from which a bride might choose. Her location choice and season will dictate many parameters for what is possible and what is unwise in the out-of-doors for her wedding and reception needs. Certainly the size of the wedding list might be in the range of 200 guests for a formal event, a mid-range of 50 to 150, or a semiformal more intimate gathering of 25 to 50 guests. Outdoor terrain can present beautiful focal points for the exchange of vows, seated dining, or even the portable dance floor site.

An outdoor setting may also have difficult challenges that will require ingenuity to overcome aesthetically and safely. The more safety issues the outdoor area presents, the less likely that the bride will want many young children on the guest list. Among such concerns would be hillsides, steep stairs, open water, loose boulders, large fountains, fenced-in animals—particularly steers, horses, llamas, etc.—bridges, and so on. Uneven terrain that makes walking difficult for ladies in high heels or for the elderly grandparents of the bride and groom may well need to be addressed.

With problems aside, outdoor weddings and receptions are splendid sensory experiences for everyone on the guest list, not to mention the wedding pair. People relax outdoors and nature's influence is the reason.

Sunshine, moonlight, starlight, pleasing sounds of birds or moving water, the scent of blossoms, beautiful colors and textures of fresh grass and flowers . . . why wouldn't a couple choose to hold their wedding in the beauty of the outdoors? And space! Outdoor areas of private homes, garden estates, country clubs, farms, ranches, and resort hotels can accommodate not only more guests comfortably than indoors, but provide for a wider range of possible activities in the fresh air. And nature is romantic!

Outdoor settings inspire nature's colors, forms, and imagery in decorative accents for the wedding and reception. The old-world elegance of the classical gazebo at left is complemented by the draped table in the foreground. Heirloom lace, a framed portrait of the bride, fine china, and roses complete the look.

At right, reception party favors made of crepe paper have secret wishes for each guest from the bride and groom hidden inside. They are charming thank yous echoed by tiny gift boxes with a single chocolate. Roses grace the china, the party favor, and the box. Stemware for the reception can be fanciful when decorated with embossing, handpainting, or gilding. A variety of designs in harmonizing colors is pretty.

In all things of Nature there is something of the Marvelous —Aristotle

From every view, the bride, her attendants, and her decorative style signature in floral and table design should be apparent. The relaxed curving forms in nature that we see in blossom petals, leaves, vines, tree lines, and rolling hill shapes can be repeated for harmony that pleases. From a gown's lacy hem line to the breezy pouf of a veil or a beribboned wreath of flowers, an outdoor wedding celebrates the freedom of airy spaces and the diversity of regional foliage.

Wherever a natural focal point can be emphasized or an arrangement using natural materials can be created, play up the freshness and simplicity of the out-of-doors. Let the flowers and foliage have the style "voice." That means all other elements, such as the texture and color of the shell frame above right, reflect nature components. Keep candles white or neutral so they support the wedding flower colors that the bride will have found abundant in nature.

COUNTRY

*C*ountry living is all about expanding into nature's space. Instead of enjoying a small garden, or even a patio planter in the city, the country has a bigger canvas to paint on visually. Imagery is in park or meadow expanses of lush grass, trees to be enjoyed from a distance, and perhaps even an inviting woods or an expanse of water. There is room to move in the country, room enough for everyone.

The air is fresher, the grass truly is greener, and instead of a few flowers in a bordered bed, we can enjoy whole meadows of fragrance and color. What a beautiful space for an outdoor wedding and its accompanying reception. Music floats on a gentle breeze. Photographers grab wide-angle lenses to record photos for an atmospheric wedding album.

Brides who have the expanse of a country setting to plan an outdoor wedding can use the entire landscape to style advantage. Nature has its own opulence. Stage guest seating to take in a lovely meadow or craggy mountain vista, a graceful bridge or stairway, a lily pond or cascade, or the commanding architecture of a stately country home.

Long-distance travel for guests to a country retreat may be a consideration, but expensive parking is not likely to be a problem. Rake the corral clean and decorate it with ribbons.

Holding a wedding and reception on an estate property is like painting a picture on the largest canvas you can find. Though a veranda with an impressive balustrade would be a fine place for the exchange-of-vows ceremony, this bride decided to leave it for the musicians and dancers. She opted to have a delicate and symbolic shelter created for the officiant to conduct the sacred part of the service with she and the groom and their immediate party. All other attendants gather just outside of it. For the benefit of the photographer to stage the best views for close ups and panoramic styling, before-ceremony photos were taken. Folding chairs and tables were given elegant treatment with yards of draped and ribbon-sashed coverings that were allowed to puddle on the grass.

The beautifully manicured lawns and gardens of this impressive mansion were ideal for enhancing an already magnificent setting. If such a country home is not available to you for your wedding or reception, consider a country churchyard, a country bed and breakfast, or a remote resort property. Particularly in their off seasons, such commercial places are eager for your business and reasonable with their prices and accommodations for your events and your guests. A relaxing swim after an evening of dining and dancing is a lovely way for your guests to wind down after an all-day and all-evening series of festivities. Weddings held on country properties often include providing comfortable and convenient lodging right on the premises where all celebration events take place.

Whatever the religious wedding traditions that call for sacred rituals, many couples feel that their Maker is nowhere more present for solemnizing their vows than in nature. Weddings outdoors are set with the grass, trees, birds, and flowers to support the natural theme. Brides who choose it decorate with nature items. At left, flowers are twined with grapevine and ivy around the *huppah* posts, while below the "posts" themselves are young saplings cut for the purpose.

Jewish wedding ceremonies not held in the synagogue will maintain ritual expectations with the traditional canopy, called a *huppah*, where the rabbi will conduct the exchange of vows for the bridal couple. The groom and other males wear their *yarmulkes*, head coverings, out of respect for the sacred presence of the Almighty. Note the embellished *huppah* at right.

Focal points for flower arrangements and gifts need not be elaborate or outrageously expensive to be elegant. Related colors, simple flowers, even a decorated tray table, bench, or love seat can be pressed into service for a gift table, or a cake or champagne display.

For an intimate garden wedding and reception, a patio, porch, deck, or hotel veranda can be decorated with the bride's choice of colors in ribbons and flowers. Some couples prefer to keep every design element as simple as possible, as a reflection of their life-style approach and to focus on the purity of their simple vows to love and cherish one another for a lifetime.

Ideas for unique approaches to styling details require only imagination and a spirit of adventure. With a modest investment, familiar items and materials or the unusual combinations of them make an extraordinary style statement. Bright red and orange are unique for a flower girl's dress. A crystal "kiss" favors a guest's stemware. Chill it before pouring in adult's clear punch, to keep it cold, before taking home as a bride's gift. A glass lantern protects the flame of a single taper. Fill it part way with rose petals, and seat on a turf-filled pan for a unique centerpiece. For a winter wedding, replace the petals with holly, mistletoe, or pinecones. A drift of white cotton or Christmas garlands sprinkled with "snowflakes" replace fresh grass for winter dazzle. Tuck rice, roses, or gifts in tiny bags.

pirited style

The spirited style is expressive and unique with a decided departure from the expected; the surprise element is taken perhaps to the point of joyful abandon. This bride and groom are sure to share their wedding celebration with exuberant loved ones—which might well include children, dogs, a steer, a horse—or a vintage car, plane, or boat. The prized photo album will include styled pictures of formally and informally posed wedding party members and guests, as well as candids of special moments. The spirited couple may arrange for several photographers, each with a style mission to capture on film. For example, one might be engaged to shoot only color, while another uses sepia tone or black and white. Assign attendants to support each photographer so no one is omitted. A spirit of fun and creativity sets the mood for this wedding style that is perhaps a bit sassy and will doubtless exude "attitude."

RANCH

*T*here's little to limit the joys of the great outdoors on a ranch. The great open spaces, the hard work, good times, and healthy attitude lay the groundwork for a wedding styled out-of-the-ordinary. There will be children on hand, and domesticated animals to add their beauty, grace, or delightfully awkward amusement. Rustic touches abound, for the ranch is a workplace. The spirited bride can make her statement by artfully combining rough and sturdy elements with her own sense of feminine style.

Folks on the farm or on the ranch are more likely to feature sunflowers and daisies with their rambling country roses than they are lilies and long stems. Their connection to nature is an intimate one, rather like you'd include a good friend. They know about nature.

Whether a pleasure or working ranch, the idea is not to take yourself too seriously, but to get the job done. It matters to have fun doing it, too. Fashions may be formal, semiformal, or themed, such as cowboy, homespun, or decorating with heirlooms. It's that spirited attitude that makes such weddings so unique.

Posing the wedding couple before a prized barn, corral, or wagon-wheel bridge sets the rustic tone. These portraits express the hard work and serious commitment of people who work outdoors, or those who wish they did, when they come out to the country on getaway weekends. Rustic wood, trees and flowers, space, animals, and big sky are the spirited style elements this bride and groom will employ for their day.

Just because a flower is not an exotic variety does not mean it can't be given exotic style treatment. Style purple and gold for drama in complementary colors.

This bride's crowning glory is natural and totally dependent upon flowers and foliage grown on the farm or the ranch. Her unpretentious appearance celebrates an attitude of pleasure in all things "outdoorsy." If she plays violin, it's in bare feet.

When a spirited bride finds her man, he knows she comes with the horse. In positive spirit, he's pleased with the idea of an outdoor life. While some ranch brides choose a traditional romantic hairstyle, others want a look that is as natural and unique as feathers and curls with their pearls.

A ranch wedding and reception will include swing dancing, fun foods, and a pleasing blend of dressing up and acting up. The fun of set-ups for photography that plays upon the bride or groom's hobby swapping antics will bring smiles to everyone who peruses the wedding album. The elements of formal weddings, as in the formal attire, draped organza through the trees and on the log "pew" symbols at right, for example, combine easily with relaxed floral design rules for nature's bounty of sunflowers. Symmetrically arranged seating with an ancient tree for a dramatic backdrop for staging the vows ceremony is "church" in the outdoors, not at all too stuffy on the ranch.

Though the ranch bride may often select a traditional gown with veil and train, she may wear white cowboy boots to walk across the pasture and her groom may opt for a tux styled with Western yoke and a matching cowboy hat. Her attendants may wear traditional gowns, or they may appear in dressy broomstick skirts made of linen or velvet. Groomsmen will likely wear Western jackets and matching cowboy hats. The ranch bride, who wears the traditional Cinderella gown she's dreamed of since girlhood, will want lace or tiny flowers or many petticoats to fulfill that dream, just as if her ranch wedding site were a palace.

A ranch bride is less likely to be sparkling with myriad diamonds or hundreds of pearls on her gown. Ethereal lace and wispy folds catch the slightest breeze. Her hair may be styled as nature intended or romantically contrived as for a bygone era. She doesn't worry about showing some "girl next door" sweetness in a blend of earth-bound yet nostalgic romance. Her beauty-secret embellishments are her health and joy in being wed to the love of her life. She has an unshakeable faith in matters of the land and the heart. She's comfortable in her own skin—anywhere. There is elegance —perhaps shared with a favored pet who may sport styling details of its own.

However formal the attire of her wedding party, the ranch or farm bride will ask her photographer to style the photos in natural poses in a favorite outdoor setting—perhaps where her new husband proposed. An outdoor wedding and reception can have a sports theme as well. Whether hunting, boating, fishing, or golfing, include some stylish props such as stuffing fishing kreels or golf bags with flowers. Golf clubs and other gear celebrate a pleasure that the couple plan to enjoy together in their future. Saddles and horses for the equestrian or rodeo couple can receive special styling treatment too. The bachelor or bachelorette party preceeding the wedding festivities could certainly include a friendly game of golf, tennis, or a horseback ride on the grounds of the ranch.

This bride and her father photograph exemplifies the outdoor wedding party portraits that express their genuine love for one another and their comfort with their ranch life-style. The bride is as approachable by her wedding guests as the land is to the sky.

A delightful mix of formal and informal style elements is apparent here. Her gown, veil, and her father's tuxedo are classic black and white formal.

The decorated horse-jumping standards act as "pew" markers for the wedding party to pass between rows of their guests. The split-rail fence and equestrian ranch setting are all inextricably incorporated. In lieu of a formal church canopy or classic arch, a rough-hewn canopy draped with organdy and open to the dramatic sky makes an ideal ranch-style focal point for the exchanging of the vows. The garden and horse trailers, barns and farm implements only add to the ranch theme and should be enjoyed.

Poses for group photos of a wedding party include a carpet of flower petals on the grass and cowboy hats!

FAMILY

*F*amilies are all important to the spirited bride. She is likely to plan her theme around the individuals she most wants to honor with participation her dream-come-true wedding and reception. No effort will be too much trouble for her in making loved individuals feel special, whether they be toddlers or elders.

Styling the ensembles for children and other attendants is a great part of the excitement. The attention to detail in the darling dresses and hairpieces of these twin flower girls will delight family and guests. For her own style statement, the bride's hair is coifed princesslike, with looping curls piled high and accented with pearls. Her veil sweeping down beneath them is a romantic-era style beautifully complemented by the little girls, dressed alike in white. She will enjoy posing with them and with other family members and friends for her wedding album. The family-oriented bride makes certain each guest is photographed.

The unexpected in children's innocent curiosity about what it is and where the ritual garter is to be found makes for a keepsake family photo to be smiled about for years. Record also the groomsmen who were college friends of the groom reunited for the wedding.

A balcony or second story window provides a photographer with a unique point of view. The fun of staging a bride with her attendants twirling their skirts to a lilting tune shows in a photo that will be memorable in the wedding album. The scene could have been taken from a Renaissance oil painting. The formal garden setting with its pavers, borders, and fountain inspired the idea.

The bride, her mother, new mother-in-law, and attendants begin a ritual with champagne or a non-alcoholic beverage, so the children can be included. Each woman toasts the bride with a special wish for her future happiness. Following all toasts, each breaks their glass by tossing it into a fireplace or out-of-doors. Tradition dictate they should never be used for lesser reason.

Bridal rituals are so important to family and friends as bonding memories that it's the wise bride who includes the youngest to the oldest of her own family and her new husband's. A special small bouquet intended only as a keepsake can be tossed in a little ritual aside from the tossing of her wedding bouquet to herald the next bride among her single female family members.

May the rest of your lives be like a bed of roses...without the thorns. —unknown

When the spirited bride and groom include their loved ones, everyone gets into the act from toddlers to dog companions. A collar decorated for the occasion with flowers that complement her bouquet—and of course the pet shines in wedding photos. Some couples even have their dogs as ring bearers with symbolic rings tied with ribbons to their collars. Child or puppy, the less-than-well-behaved get attention.

ECLECTIC

*E*clectic is the most spirited bride of all. She will borrow styling ideas from a variety of sources and combine them with her personal air of confidence and savvy. Her wedding and reception will be like no other because her personality reigns.

The eclectic bride is often sophisticated in her tastes for the unusual. She has a "thinking outside the box" approach to everything in her life. Breaking rules doesn't occur to her because she just doesn't notice rules in the first place. But even if she is bursting with sassy attitude, she exhibits enviable class.

With a taste for beauty and an innovative mind, what she is attracted to in details from classical formal to Victorian, shabby-chic style, all natural, or severely minimalist will be reinterpreted by her wedding vision. Her conservative guests will gape. At least she hopes they will! The eclectic bride will make every effort to create her personal breathtaking style with attitude.

Combining elements in unusual ways is her signature. Green apples or green grapes with pink roses, wildflowers, or herbs in crystal vases tied with black satin ribbon? Of course, why not?

The spirited bride may be the one who marries an equally eclectic man. They may have divergent tastes, cultural and religious or life-style differences, conflicting careers, separate hobbies and interests, and even intend for career reasons to live in different localities and commute to be together, but does that intimidate her? Not a bit! Life is full of adventurous things for her to try and to accomplish with finesse. The eclectic bride's wedding will reflect her confidence, daring, and vibrant spirit!

Eclectic focal points are "over the top" design statements. A cake is not like anyone else's wedding cake. It will be styled with attitude toward the glamorous, sentimental, fresh and natural, or wild and wonderful.

Where a wall backdrop seems too ordinary for a baby grand piano, a display of gifts, champagne, or dramatic wedding cake, the spirited eclectic bride will have a memorable fresh idea to solve the style challenge.

She may string stemmed flowers and hang them in rows, staple a fabulous fabric to a lattice and trim it with fringe, ribbon streamers, beads, or swags of lace.

Mardi Gras is a time of wild abandon in many cities of the world, so why not propose a wedding cake design that is deliciously whimsical and quite as mad as the sweet star of a hatter's tea party. Meringue spirals for a topper surmount a carefully styled, tipsy effect for tiers that appear to whirl and distort with the power of centrifical force. The unlikely cake appears to dance on its plate as if captured in a moment of Mardi Gras revelry, bound to bring smiles. The flower, harlequin diamond, and buttonlike details of colored frosting are cake-decorating artistry at its most unique.

A Mardi Gras season wedding is exciting to plan. Table place settings in punchy colors, such as designing with Mardi Gras's traditional purple, red, gold, and green, can snap with lively texture and vibrant detail, including masks to be given to each guest. Everything else about their wedding and reception will also make a unique statement that combines the expected with the totally unexpected in attitude. The spirited eclectic bride's hair color, cut, and style will be unique, perhaps a bit edgy, or severe, yet feminine. She may incorporate beads, braids, hair ornaments, or feathers. Food presentations may dazzle.

Some bridal parties will be so natural and relaxed as to have all of the women attendants wear sandals or bright thongs befitting the wedding theme. Color coordinated nail polish and toe rings, ankle bracelets and a little "sparkle" body lotion add the glitz.

The bride will choose her footwear carefully as it is bound to be seen by the reception guests during the garter ritual between her and her attentive groom. As the wedding reception draws to a close, their individual lives merge into what they will make of the many responsibilities and privileges of their marriage.

A woman's love of pretty shoes is notorious. The spirited bride may choose a traditional white satin pump with fine silk hose or she may do what was unthinkable for her grandmother—wear open-toed shoes to her dressy wedding—without nylon hose! Some brides opt for ballet-style wedding slippers.

Or a bride may insist that one style of shoe and dress be worn for the wedding ceremony, and another more relaxed and comfortable ensemble be changed into for the reception. This is a more common choice when the after-wedding festivities move outdoors to a luau, a home barbeque, or a beachside clam bake.

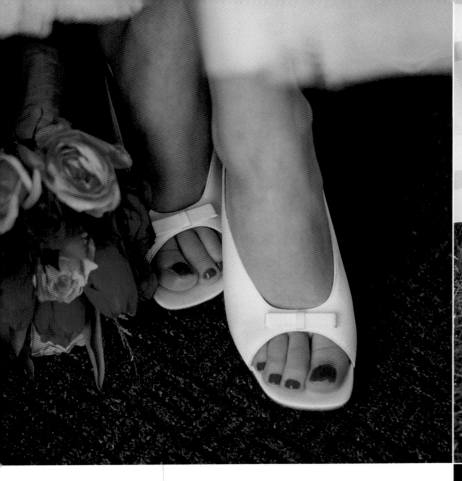

Every bride deserves a Cinderella day — Caroll Shreeve

After the wedding ceremony, the groom stops following his bride's lead. They move into a true life partnership.

Following all the planning and creating of every detail of their wedding, newlyweds relax and enjoy their honeymoon. Now all of their love and planning can go into their future together. They will treasure the happy memories of their special day for anniversaries to come.

About the Author

Sy Snarr, born and reared on an Idaho farm, knew by her early teens that she wanted to be a photographer. Gaining camera skills by snapping photos of her farm surroundings, Sy began photographing weddings for family and friends about fifteen years ago.

She used a friend's Hasselblad® camera once and was hooked; she had to have one of her own. Her business grew to include engagement photos, bridals, weddings, families, children, and farm animals.

She enjoys photographing weddings because they are such happy occasions. "I try to capture something unique and different about the spontaneity and excitement of each wedding I photograph," she says. Sy also credits photography with some of the great people she has met and the many friends she has made. Mother of four children and grandmother of two, she enjoys traveling in many parts of the world, quilting, reading, going to movies, and spending good times with her family and close friends. Her wedding photographs sell regularly to a major style publisher.

This book is dedicated to my son Zach.

ACKNOWLEDGMENTS

I wish to thank Jo Packham for her invitation to do this book and Chapelle Ltd. for the use of studio facilities for style photography. I also thank Chapelle's Caroll McKanna Shreeve for her contribution of writing the styling text to accompany my photographs and to give brides and their mothers ideas for special wedding memories of their own.

Photographed by Sy Snarr

Additional Photography by:

Anthony Lordemann: 3(u)(r), 12, 16(ul), 20(l), 20(ll), 26(ul), 45(ur), 46(ur), 54(lr), 106, 136(ll)

Hazen: 13, 111(ll), 116(u), 117, 118, 121, 130(l), 138(lr)

Ken Ring: 94(m)

Kevin Dilley: 16, 20(r)(ul), 18(ll), 26(ll), 32(u), 33(lr), 34, 35(r), 36(r), 38(lu)(ll), 40, 41(ul)(ll)(ur), 42(ur)(l), 45(lr), 47(l), 54(ll), 56(r), 58(l), 62, 69, 70(l)(r), 80(ul)(ll), 83, 87(r), 88(ul)(lr) 89(l), 94(r), 105(r), 138(ul)

Luciana Pampalone: 52(l), 53(r), 102(r), 103

Scherry Tibbins Moore: 114, 122(ll)(ur), 123

Scott Zimmerman: 16–17, 137

Thomas Hardy: 47(r), 141

Photodisk: 1, 25(r), 38(r), 42, 49(r), 52, 54(ul), 56(ul), 73, 97, 100, 101(l), 102(l), 126(r), 129, 130(r), 135(lr), 136(ul)

Artville: 41(lr)

APPRECIATION

For the use of their products, the publishers wish to thank:

A1 Paper Design
3117 West Twelve Mile
Berkeley, MI 48072
Photo album p.32

Jaynie Maxfield c/o Ambrosia
115 South 2625 East
Layton, UT 84041
Cakes pp.16–17, 115

Barreveld International
3027 Route 9
Cold Spring, NY 10516
Dove bowl p.33(r)

Brioni Art Glass
PO Box 1045
Palm Harbor, FL 34682
Stemware p.80(ul)

Dancing Bubbles
4500 E. Speedway Blvd. Suite 41
Tucson, AZ 85712
Bubble wand p.86

Desert Heart, Inc.
2220 E. Colfax Ave.
Denver, CO 80206
Necklace and Bracelet p.38 (ll)(far
right in photo)

Elegant Gourmet
11836 NE 112th Street
Kirkland, WA 98033
Rose gift box p.64(ul), Sucker p.86

Empress Arts
1455 Monterey Pass Rd. #108
Montery Park, CA 91754
www.empressarts.com
Lamp p.136(ul)

English Card Co.
PO Box 296
Levittown, NY 11756-9998
Photo album p.32, Flower from card
p.34(l), Heart from card p.47(l),
Nature heart from card p.58(l)

Gloriosa
395 Main Street PO Box 369
Ashfield, MA 01330
Photo album p.32

Hanah Silk
5155 Myrtle Ave.
Eureka, CA 95503
Glass chocolate kiss p.105(ul)

Katherine's Collection
PO Box 951185
Cleveland, OH 44193
Heart box p.136(r), Tussy-mussy
p.46(lr), Album p.32(ur)

John Martinez
754 West Cahoon
Ogden, UT 84401
Chocolate box p.80(ll)

Lavana Shurtliff
PO Box 178
Mt. Pleasant, MI 48804-0178
Bracelet p.105(r)

Max & Lucy
5444 E. Washington St. Suite 3
Phoenix, AZ 85034
www.maxandlucy.com
Card p.86

Meri Meri
PO Box 954
Belmont, CA 94002
Shoe from card p.139(ll)

Motel Deluxe Inc.
833 Washington St. 2nd Floor, #1
New York, NY 10014
Card p.93

Rachel Scharmon
801-479-9398
Bracelet p.38(ll)(far right in photo)

Robert Held Art Glass
2130 Pine St.
Vancouver BC Canada V6J 5B1
Glass heart p.33(l)

Segev
538 Lorimer St. #1L
Brooklyn, NY 11211
Stemware jewerly p.80(ul)

Tops Malibu
PO Box 2673
Eugene, OR 97402
Papier mâché gift ball p.93(ur)

Two Women
1108 Howard St.
San Francisco, CA 94103
Glass hearts p.33(lr)

Two's Company
30 Warren Place
Mount Vernon, NY 10550
Cake plate p.87(m), Red gem heart
frame p.88(lr)

Zodax
14040 Arminta St.
Panorama City, CA 91402
www.zodax.com
Cup p.88(ul)

Tracy Porter c/o Zrike Co.
8 Thornton Rd.
Oakland, NJ 07436
Candle p.42(l), Plate p.88(lr), Forks
p.93, Glassware p.93(lr), Stemmed
dish p.105(ul)

INDEX

Acknowledgments 142

Autumn 62, 78–81

Classic Style 9–59

Country Style 28, 96–105

Eclectic Style 132–140

Family Style 124–131

Floral Styling 6, 8–29, 31, 38, 42, 45–46, 49–54, 56–78, 80, 82–85, 88–91, 100–104, 111–113, 117–118, 120, 122–124, 126, 128–130, 132–135, 144

Food Styling 21–22, 70–71, 74–75, 77, 79, 85, 132–133

Formal Style 12–27, 50–59

Gift for Guest 20, 32–33, 36, 41, 46, 49, 52–53, 64, 86–87, 93, 102, 105, 136

Guest Book 32, 38, 87

Hairstyling 26–27, 42, 60–61, 64–65, 69, 94, 115, 118, 123–125

Natural Style 9, 60–105

Outdoor Style 75, 90–95, 116–124

Photo Styling 10, 12–14, 18, 24–25, 27, 39, 43–45, 47, 54, 58–59, 76, 89, 94–98, 100, 104, 106–111, 113–115, 116–128, 137–141, 144

Ranch Style 28, 110–123

Ring Pillow 33, 48, 89

Romantic Style 9, 28–29, 32–35, 44, 83

Seasonal Style 62–89

Sophisticated Style 50, 52, 57–58, 82

Spirited Style 9, 106–140

Spring Style 62, 64–68

Summer 62, 72–77

Table Styling 4–5, 16, 20–21, 26–27, 30–31, 33–38, 40–42, 46, 48, 52–54, 56, 70–71, 74–75, 78, 80, 84, 86–88, 92–93, 98, 102, 105, 134, 136

Wedding Attire 12, 18, 24, 27–29, 35, 38, 44–45, 47, 58–61, 64–69, 76–77, 82, 90, 94–95, 97. 100–102, 104, 111, 113–124, 126–131, 137–138, 140

Wedding Cake 3, 12, 15–17, 19, 23, 25–26, 30–31, 38, 45–46, 54–56, 63, 72, 78–79, 81, 84, 103, 135, 137

Winter 62, 82–89, 105